# THE PORTAGE POETRY SERIES

Series Titles

*Lake, River, Mountain*
Mark B. Hamilton

*The Blue Divide*
Linda Nemec Foster

*The Watching Sky*
Judy Brackett Crowe

*Let It Be Told in a Single Breath*
Russell Thorburn

*Talking Diamonds*
Linda Nemec Foster

*The Green Vault Heist*
David Salner

*There is a Corner of Someplace Else*
Camden Michael Jones

*Everything Waits*
Jonathan Graham

*We Are Reckless*
Christy Prahl

*Always a Body*
Molly Fuller

*Bowed As If Laden With Snow*
Megan Wildhood

*Silent Letter*
Gail Hanlon

*New Wilderness*
Jenifer DeBellis

*Holding My Selves Together: New and Selected Poems*
Margaret Rozga

*Lost and Found Departments*
Heather Dubrow

*Marginal Notes*
Alfonso Brezmes

*The Almost-Children*
Cassondra Windwalker

*Meditations of a Beast*
Kristine Ong Muslim

Praise for

## Lake, River, Mountain

"The last poem in Mark B. Hamilton's *Lake, River, Mountain*, a lovely near-haiku, reads: 'A mountain lily / shines underfoot in the snow. / Life is this close.' Throughout the book, he holds life as close as the shining flower, especially in the rich series of poems about his journey by kayak retracing the Lewis and Clark Trail and observing their rate of travel. This is a wise, tough, and joyful collection. 'How wonderful the Earth! / How sweet the scent of this red slate beach.'"

—Ann Fisher-Wirth
author of *Paradise Is Jagged*
co-editor of *The Ecopoetry Anthology*

"With poetic grace, Mark B. Hamilton brings life's past portages to the present, never to be forgotten. *Lake, River, Mountain* expresses the ongoing grandeur of rediscovering relationships with past landscapes; only Mark has experienced these episodes and retells these crossings with honesty and humility as he brings them into being again."

—Rich Clow
author of *Spotted Tail: Warrior and Statesman*
Professor Emeritus, University of Montana

"If Lewis & Clark had a poet with them, it would have been Mark Hamilton. Visually captive, thought provoking and inspiring. Hamilton captures the feel of a long journey on the water with *Lake, River, Mountain*."

—Norm Miller
founder of Missouri River Paddlers

"Mark Hamilton travels in a world made of metaphor. On the water paddling his kayak on an epic journey or on land, camping, he sees what others might only look at, finds the unexpected relationships. Inanimate things have awareness: '...the river feels everything passing/ and knows of its approach.' Camping, 'all night my tent blinks with lightning/ flaps and sags under the immense gray sky.' All his senses are fully awake, and ours are awakening as we journey with him 'upstream on this difficult river/ learning to accept, learning to avoid'—a metaphor for life itself."

—Grace Butcher
editor (retired) and founder of *The Listening Eye*
Professor Emerita, Kent State University–Geauga

# Lake,
# River,
# Mountain

Mark B. Hamilton

CORNERSTONE PRESS
UNIVERSITY OF WISCONSIN-STEVENS POINT

Cornerstone Press, Stevens Point, Wisconsin 54481
Copyright © 2024 Mark B. Hamilton
www.uwsp.edu/cornerstone

Printed in the United States of America by
Point Print and Design Studio, Stevens Point, Wisconsin

Library of Congress Control Number: 2023943635
ISBN: 978-1-960329-18-9

Cornerstone Press titles are produced in courses and internships offered by the
Department of English at the University of Wisconsin–Stevens Point.

DIRECTOR & PUBLISHER              EXECUTIVE EDITORS
Dr. Ross K. Tangedal             Jeff Snowbarger, Freesia McKee

EDITORIAL DIRECTOR               SENIOR EDITORS
Ellie Atkinson                   Brett Hill, Grace Dahl

PRESS STAFF
Chloe Cieszynski, Carolyn Czerwinski, Zoie Dinehart, Kirsten Faulkner, Kenzie
Kierstyn, Maddy Mauthe, Natalie Reiter, Lauren Rudesill, Anthony Thiel

*To Glover Davis,*
*a fine man, teacher, and poet*

Also by Mark B. Hamilton:

*Upstream*
*OYO: The Beautiful River*
*100 Miles of Heat*
*Confronting the Basilisk*
*Earth Songs*

# Contents

# Lake, River, Mountain

# A Geography of the Heart

*—to Phil Brown and Mark McMahon*

On orange avenues
of organonymous skin
where young women
lean in doorways of faded
dungaree blue and red
tin rusted-roofed houses,
where cool spaces
shelter hammocks
near open windows
of breezy, starry nights,

young men walk on dusty roads
beneath their straw hats
to endless-hour breakfasts
as iridescent roosters crow
and strong women comb
white chickens, closing gently
the brown shaggy
fence-slatted gates,

days floating in the heat
stripped down to a collapse
of sandy shallows, the sun
sitting into its curve
of beach, the long horizon,
our friendships tilting back
into moonwalk light
far from Georgetown bars
and rural separateness,

pool tables rising grand
and green with reggae
as we drank gulps
with new-eyed people

in the open cafés, lime
trimmed and rum-coordinated
with songs by Jimmy Cliff
and Marley Mann,

the surf folding back
like glass onto the dunes
near the Governor's mansion
where anthems were sung
with those concerns
of young and questioning men,

the local island toughs
swarming on motorbikes
like sparks around the fire,
the stars circling
above like insects
in the unsleepable air.

## Uncle Lowell

My father would visit
each Thursday from his work
to grocery shop for my great-uncle Lowell,
bald-headed bachelor still in love
with his magnolia tree, pink-white blossoms
just like the ladies walking
beyond the hedge
of his wide rocking porch.

Ringing the bell,
rapping on the old screen door,
my father would stand
expectantly in suit, short hair and tie.
And in a very few minutes a voice
would rise up like tin
and fall, slightly past syllables
like bits of shale sliding
into the air gently off the roof.

"I'm comin', Hal!" we'd hear, "I'm comin'!"

And sure enough,
not more than two or three minutes
would pass before he'd turn that corner
from back kitchen to dining room,
"I'm comin'!" rising like steam
from a locomotive
hissing its brakes in a small town
as he towered into the foyer.
His years of generosity
seemed a solid engine,
his quick blue-gray eyes,
four-day whiskers and bright smile
shining with effort above his vested suit
with tobacco stains on broad lapels

and his soft hands that fluttered
like pendants above the door latch,

tentatively, as if time
were to be spent slowly
with family and other gentle folk
at meals below a Tiffany lamp,
along the carved wooden table
of his eventful, domestic life.

# When I Was a Child

all the trees
carried blue dresses,

all my hurts
curved and strung
by roots and flowers
in the breezes beneath
a banyan tree.

In the coolness
of a soothing fountain
I would sit drifting
in the mist on the steps
of a bronze sculpture,
its gnarl of dogs
circling a man
green with muscle,
snapping at his heart.

A wounded stag
arrow-pierced gasped
above the flashing fountain,
saddened by the whirl
Manship had made
of the sacrificed
and of the freed,

the fountain
cool and brimming
with bronze and the splashing
of green flowers.

## Considering Flight

I was scattered,
struggling to collect
and launch
like a barn swallow
from its nest,

from its cup of mud
to swoop the sky.

It wanted to go. I could see it.

It wanted to leave
not from weakness, nor any lack
as a way of escape—
not from some crisis of identity,

but from the ledge
it needed that trajectory
to tug its small body
into flight.

Like learning algebra
on a square card table
going forward was not the equation
of regret, moving on
was not a loss
from the away.

Altered to apparent emptiness
explanations were
the reason,
one's self the recognition
in that collapsing moment
when the dark wings joined.

# Departing the Mandans

Thick with stars,
the sky flecked with origins of the Milky Way,
I plan a fragile constellation.

Sand bars like swimmers at sunset,
shoulders glistening gold and speckled tan,

the Missouri River passing
with questions of self, history, and time
I am willing to know.

I pack "Gander" with provisions, medical kit, books,
stove, and charts at the historic site of Fort Mandan.

In a glassed-in gift shop,
my kayak had stayed for winter's thaw
and the returning geese.

Chief Black Cat had spoken with winter stories,
offering survival to Lewis and Clark with trade and maps.

I wait for FedEx,
for a graphite, feather-light paddle as strong
and as supple as a blacksnake,

Gander launching down a long log skid
over sharp rocks piled high at the river's edge.

Sand bars and islands
approach in their low earthen skins
of early April air.

Again, I'm paddling upstream on this difficult river
learning to accept, learning to avoid.

Buzzards drift up
from spring-green thorn bushes, shifting
on their dark wings.

Why suffer the bad when the good is so near?
Even a small poem is a joyful happiness!

Little waves and cans
wash up onto the beach with voices
strung with beginnings.

All day, I paddle with questions leaning right
and left along the answering sands.

From reeds, a coot peers
from beneath the rain on its splayed toes,
feeding on a mat of flowers.

All night my tent blinks with lightning,
flaps and sags under the immense gray sky.

# In His Arms

a cradle
of toy things

a carpenter's bench
with bolts and pegs
that a hammer
pounded through

brightly colored
plastic sails
the doing
when there was
a lack of him

each squall
replicated
as the safest place
I knew

# A Father's Father

I think he was
reconstructing
with increments of the past,
each shot glass
an upside down city
bursting into flame
when he asked,
"Was that enough?"

I once heard the oak say,
"Everyone falls asleep
because the wind sways
my roots so gently."

He was the sunrise
once a year, a loud voice
in the kitchen,
pageant plays, football games,
pancakes and thick bacon
on the wall-to-wall carpeting,

and a memory
of a wife who had died young,
her son awakening to a leather
belt before breakfast
to cook and wash dishes
and do other household chores.

Living with fists by twelve
he learned the exact symmetry
of balsa wood airplanes
intricately willed into flight,

the basement walls pinned
with track shirts and blue prints

of fixed-winged models
built with razor blades and glue,

where my father's father
hanged himself years later,
dying not from a heart attack
as I was told.

# Surviving April on Sakakawea Lake

How huge the wind
and raw the dance of pelting ice—
those bouncing beans of hail.

Even songbirds hesitate, turkey calls and other
little sounds scattering in the prairie grass.

A flittering of finches
into the bending straw of winter's fallen spaces,
each settling out of sight.

How the wicked winds do strengthen the wary,
yet frighten all my deep, deaf parts.

Scrunched into one
dry corner of the tent—two days
fair and five days foul.

I hide in a nook, a small hook of cove,
accepting whatever comfort remains:

the woodless prairie;
a clutch of coal under smoldering smoke;
and the wild brant's wing,

to lift my spirit from this blustery camp,
from this huddled site with rain trenching past.

Wet and cold and gray
I circle words in a book of words,
nothing more.

A precious rock weighs down the tent
nearly floating away with me in it reading *The Journals*,

where Lewis and Clark had camped
with these same northwest winds—the fear
a descendant of fatigue.

In stillness, I learn not to be the target, nor the center
of these tearing winds. Not the origin to be altered.

My emptiness widens
into a ring of warmth that surrounds.
How does this happen?

Tent stakes get blown out from under their rocks.
I dash out for bigger ones. Another sleepless night.

The candle flame warms
my thick woolen socks. And how delicious
these thin strips of beef jerky:

tough and stringy, angular and stretched out flat
like a bat's wing, brittle and a little bit salty.

In bed clothes, the waves
stumble out onto the beach in their white caps,
scarves, and jagged slippers.

Gulls wheel above in spray, flying like hope
in a veering wind that points to change.

I roll up the tent,
pack away all my soggy gear and launch
back into the curving claws

to paddle on the river beast, beneath its blue sky
coming my way, waters running fast.

A black-tipped gull
mews above, sounding like a cat knowing
its place in the sun,

my body glowing with hourly rhythms,
shoulders passing in conversation with golden stones.

The lands of the Assiniboine
are haunted by buffalo grazing on the hills
near New Town, North Dakota.

I pass the wild flowers nodding in place.
I pass beneath all this coyote sunshine,

and then stop to spread out
all the wet gear on river rocks,
warmed by my hosting ghosts.

# Reflections

Across the brook
there was a pond.

In the spring
I would rake out
all the dead leaves
and plant violets,

the frogs
floating in the trees
like earrings.

# Changes

Bricks stretch up
to a star,
to a white clock in the center
of a bell tower,
nights clinging to the grassy
hills moist with lank blades
drawn down from shadow.

Black and red
wings sweep
the oily river, bodies
skittering through marshes,
between corrugated sheds
zoned commercial,
buildings rising
from the wetlands,
meadows broken
into lakes of fire
that sink back
into the dark of the sleeping.

Ambushed by hunger
eyes glisten, light shreds
from skulls soaked
in the luscious blood grass
burning with dew,
heads glazed
and lifting from gut heaps.

Mountain lions slant
past in their morning hunt,
warm prey brought down
and swept away
in the muddy flood
of my awakening—a fruit
that slowly ripens.

# One Heart Moving

He knew birds and buildings,
        cars and the strengthening breeze,
white sails
so taut they could strut the sun.

He knew the wild light
        in a daisy's vibrant glance
and the studded whale's neck
that lifts from the mist like a mountain.

He knew wheat lands and the Twin Cities,
        those reflecting squares of hotel rooms,
        businessmen, and the feeling
there was no place left to go.

But he knew a little Gillespie
and the smoke curling into night forms,
                rhythms and values,
        and the toll it takes
to cross that blank and scraggling river,

the hills of the Amish, good food
and friends
        who talked from their shoes.

All these things
                he knew
        as precious aggregates of time,
                the stars scattered above
and the Red Rocks
        left undone

        as he drove towards Omaha
with that flat and rattling black bed.

# Renewal at New Town, Berthold Reservation

As if a desert
this land becomes cold quickly
when the sun goes down.

The curve of rock steps and sweeps
into buttes and cities and towns,

the prairies so green
with rain they roll emerald past
New Town's long bridge.

White pelicans watch as I paddle past:
fifty-five, plus all those wings!

I land wet and cold
and walk a mile toward The People
who are concerned for me.

They stop in old cars and talk easily
with bright, comfortable Arikara eyes.

Inside, a family
offers me a ride, a stranger
the wind to his back.

After such changes: the laundromat, the café,
and tenting near town, I relaunch my Gander body

under fast patches
of blue sky, the day becoming one long lesson
for an April storm.

Winds heap up into powerful following waves.
I lean back to surf their scowls.

Sloughing off their backs
I let the rough ones pass, hour after hour
whooshing toward a far shore.

In control, but without a choice, I rush past a man
unspeaking, waving his arms on the unreachable beach,

to land farther downwind
behind a cutbank of gnarled roots—
more miles lost than gained.

Cold winds crest over me, sunlight wedges from a cloud,
the hail bounces between mushrooms and stones.

From my tent, I watch
a pair of western grebes mirrored in the lee—
like two long-stemmed flowers

linked side to side by glances, petal to petal,
their necks entwined, bobbing in unison.

In the chirping dance
on all four feet they go splashing,
then dive, and disappear.

How wonderful the Earth!
How sweet the scent of this red slate beach.

# A Vulnerable Corollary

He could see
beyond the clock,
although his allegiance
was to the renewal of life.

He tried on the suits
of other people's eyes
and inspected the hard inner
heart of industrial floors,
each ring of wood
so concentric underfoot
it curled upward
in his head

like a friend's voice
at the end of a road:
the fluorescent space,
his job, his machine,
and the social change
no longer initiated at home.

He recoiled from this
sense of the world
with its cycle, with its
staid measure to follow,
and perceived sometimes
in fear, not with a feather
but with a hog's hair,
as the interminable trees
seemingly shed
all of his seasons' variables.

So, like the great lathe
that he once controlled,
he left that floor in rings
of darkness and light
shrugging
his broad shoulders
like a crow.

## Paddling Into the Plains of the Lakota

In the month of May
the warmth of junk scatters down a bank
like big questions to ponder.

What is this attachment to rusted and broken things?
To these square white appliances on a hill?

How easily the day
glances along passing these canyons of glass
and corrugated tin.

Like a potato bug walking up my shoelace—
they fascinate with a mask of dots.

Day after day, I trace
the shoreline with beavers on shelves of sun
like chunks of clay.

Surprised from their naps, they run through dry brush,
and dive off earthen banks like noisy pottery.

And there is jewelry, too,
in the blue sky of a heron's nest—a treasure
for just lifting the eyes.

Horses gather between fenced-off roads that loop
between bluffs toward hot, flat, and hidden towns.

Wind in the cottonwoods
rumbling like a train, cools the sweated back
and shimmers on cool water.

For there is wisdom in a driftwood fire
with frogs just beyond the light to sing it.

Camped low near the river
the gurgling snag combs the thick grass—
a hand moving through my hair.

In the morning, the noise from boxcars overwhelms
as sometimes a thought seeps up, harsh into the mind.

The single lesson
to be learned all over again—joy
is a place in the heart.

At Rocky Boy Rez,
clean socks on my water-worn feet
improve my disposition.

Sensitive to pebbles on the street, I sit on a curb
watching children returning home from school.

Taking pity, a Sioux
policeman invites me to a dinner
of stew and fry bread.

His family crowds around the table, a ladle in reach,
their voices, smiles, and their many kindnesses.

I paddle the sunrise
with pelicans stretching their wings,
awakening like water flowers.

I relax back onto the surface,
into the welcoming of my own feathery fire.

James Joyce!

Your pints
       are a curious blessing,
              the ghosts of language's laughter
ribbed into musky
       natural tales
            making fun
                  of a religion of Self.


       Of & of
like a bluebird's song
       spray painted on an alley wall,
       the unformed circuit
                a circus deformed,
       the polar bear immersed
by spine's lit swarm.

# The Bridge

I split into chunks
and scatter myself around
like an old, bad habit
floating in peripheral space.
Panhandlers
want me to stop,
but I can't,
although I sway heavily
in their emotion
of event:
the brown paper sack,
a train chugging
under its own breath,
and strangers wrapped
in fast food and cigarettes.
This bridge is as planked
and as warped as they,
penuriously huddled,
having hoboed
from Helena on a freight.
And here I am, too,
not even sure of my past.
It is not
a clear stream to me.
The river rocks
are capped in snow,
the low clouds moving
like gray travelers,
Billy Goats, everyone.

## A Friend

In tobacco nets
webs of wind
tip plants that drop with rain.

A Jamaican friend shares lunch.

Small toads pop
in a mason jar,
rebound on the casting threads.

"Wait. Be kind, mun!"
This damp earth
floods with tiger lilies.

# Dancing

Dancing
to the watercolors
on the lawn

a tree does not claim
its share of space,
but only lingers,

wrinkling its trunk,
healing the broken limb
that has even
surprised the sky.

# A Truth

I am not a perfect stranger.
I do not even see where they have lived
all of their lives.

Immersed in my own progression, I strut
proudly into this small place of summer.

The People at Wolf Point
disregard me, as I land in silence
past any sense of knowing.

A young warrior drags Gander out of the river,
everything floating away into the shadow of trees.

My give-away is a given
without me—a life preserver in the dust,
a misdirection that works.

With an open heart or not, the ritual of sharing
sweet snacks, sunglasses, a rifle, and bear spray.

Yesterday is lost,
released or abandoned. Then, accepted
in the gathering of today.

My scattered, unbroken things lay in a darkness,
discarded items in the deep shade of bushes.

Most are recovered,
but the survival rifle appears much later
with a tribal officer

who speaks of a teenager, a young mother, and about life
on the Rez. I can only say, "Thank you, Wolf Point!"

The stop revives me.
Kids wave and laugh, and free me
to find another way.

I camp on an island where bulls wallow in the dust
breaking dried trees into kindling brush.

Camped in their pasture
I'm awkward under the bright moon
brimming with white pelicans.

Wingtip to wingtip, they rasp close overhead
gliding in a long "V" toward the darkening river.

Plovers, and the snorts
of white-tailed deer in the prairie grass,
when the evening sways.

Wet sneakers on either side of the tent flaps
hold the night both inside and out.

Asleep in seconds,
I wake to the running of dew, and to sunlight
on the browsing mule deer.

They twitch, scratch and blink. Pleased to be here
with them, my discoveries are few and rare:

For chores like sewing,
a cup of cold tea is a faithful companion
in this dry and rugged country.

A mile-wide reservoir moves with the slightest of breeze,
and fresh-caught walleye truly are Lakota lobster tails.

All day, a soft murmur
of mud shale along the denuded bank
laps the captured water.

I camp in tall grass, in the rustling of high weeds
beneath the bending glow of timid moonlight.

Close-by at night,
the coyotes wrestle, yip and roll
amid mustard blossoms

in a bowling, rousing inspection—the grass flattened
by brothers and sisters of river flow and water stone.

# A Common Denominator

I dream
of a multi-storied farm
and conduits of pure sunshine,
leafy funnels opening hallways
into glass panels blossoming
with flowers of light.
I travel
inside tiny tendrils
of fiber optic stem
floor by floor to all the rows
of furrows skyward climbing.

But I live
with a hole in my pocket.

The pocket hollers, "I can take it.
I can take it all."

But a pebble whispers, "Live small.
Claim the outside."

## And Home Again

Her apartment offered a fish tank and paintings;
we fixed her VW, got her purse out of hock
and loved her art and her life and her child:
days on the beach, in the surf,
splurging on lobsters and clams in Boothbay;
we crossed three or four state lines
in that gray noise panic of downtown traffic,
everyone changing lanes at once, —the bridges,
the soot, the angry eyes and laughing faces
and the guide on the median sitting cross-legged,
waving as we sped by honking "Hello!"

Then leaving her apartment for home,
steeped with the brewed morning coffee talks.
Back across the plains, past the reapers and seagulls,
toward the divide and that Montana valley:
a small studio, Great Dane and yard fenced
with second-hand spruce posts, trains still rippling
their loud and long connections.

Outside our backdoor Ike empties his garbage,
sending it, I suppose, to Seattle or Portland
lumber yards; his cats all doing well,
the job market dim, the rent low, the walks
of gentle hands and sniffing dog along the tracks
where vases fill with wildflowers plucked
from tall grass, and nights cling to bedsheets
under the fan of humid summer, the children
straining behind the glass, barely in their seats
as an ice sweeper reglazes the rink in Chicago.

# The Missouri River Breaks

*—for Leonard Peltier,*
*and to my friends at Standing Rock*

Now, I can begin
my apology to the Lakota, as it is
my history to do so.

*All my relatives* on a journey to here, safely
in the lee of willows bent to the covering of sky,

my tent a doorway
of soft greens and tender grasses—
a slanted drum for the rain.

River banks curve through moist prairie clumps
that fall in great slabs of thick mud and mystery.

Beaver tails drop
like flat rocks onto the surface of the night
and jolt the tingling stars.

Even nighthawks carry small circles of the air
in their wings to seed tomorrow's sky.

Far from mountains
the river feels everything passing
and knows of its approach.

Plovers forage ahead, extending my vision,
improving my judgment: when to cross; when to stay.

See how the extravagant
birds are claiming the Milky Way
as their wild destination?

See how the meadowlarks bring the sunlight
to the river's edge in their slashing hearts?

A red-winged blackbird
marks all things as its territory,
celebrating the night.

Let the ridgeline rise into The People
dressed in sharp rock to sing the Great Mystery.

See how the White Cliffs
in buffalo robes are quietly conversing
with the wet sandstone?

Listen to the low ledges where the soft birds go,
and to where I'm beginning to understand why:

Life becomes a sibling
shielded in the shade of river bank
and slightly out-of-sight.

Each day seems like three. Winds continue
from the east. Birds speak, if you listen.

A flycatcher invites me
to lunch at her hidden river crossing
where deer trails intersect.

Paddling farther, I move into the crystal waters
where engineless boats are free to travel.

I am an imperfect guest
who may or may not be deaf
to sandpipers pecking.

Rising, they hover toward the starry path, silent
above the *thunk thunk* of aluminum canoes.

I stay in the shade—
a grackle floating by on its splayed wings
speaking of loneliness.

Close enough to have reached out, I might have
saved him, if I had not thought him dead.

I remain as one
in this history, but none other
would exist without it.

The night rides the scented dark and bends
the sage into whispers—into gentle promises.

Water and two pancakes.
One day to Virgelle, then Fort Benton.
Then, the Great Falls, and rest.

Young ospreys grow strong atop an old tree.
The owls in the deep cool beneath a concrete bridge.

In front of my tent
rabbits nibble on flower stems, while I
sit clapping mosquitoes.

If I am needed by nature, it is not mentioned, although
at night I hear the hooves in the dusty grasses.

## Untitled Night

I remember
her pendant, triangular and blue,
and how the world swayed
around us,

how the waves curled
over our shoulders
as we reached down
into the sand for clams,

those five hundred mile songs,
a lighted lantern, and the low tide
flickering like gold.

The world
itself was thrumming
its first new light
near brass hooks,
our warm towel hanging,

our bed
of flesh and shell
houseling around us
as the sun rose
into our room
flood slow.

# Eglise d'Auvers

*—from the painting by Vincent van Gogh*

In the wind, tongues
are grassy with earth,
words bounce back,
feet stumble
over color like dwarves
descended from steeples;

a Ferris wheel
flows madly in the sun
swinging us
back to shade, your feet
my following, all
those purple
fragile tragedies;

the path
rushing out before us,
an oven
of warm planted bulbs
flowing stone,
cowslips
tugging at our feet;

your lips
are close to the eaves
of that church, my breath
near the flowers:
those golden and purple
wings of an absolute.

## Three Dialogues, Fort Benton

"I'm a tree trimmer.
My granddad homesteaded
from Caws Creek to Dobbs.

"Had nine sons, my uncles, who drank, rioted
then sold out. None's in farming now.

"Only a brother—
hired out for room 'n board.
T'others up in Idaho, mining."

He talked of his family with a sweep of his arm,
of Indians shot right off the street.

"They'd throw 'em in the river
in any season from the steamboat pier,
day or night. No one cared.

"Can't see to neither," he said. History spooks
a person. Dreams get cut loose and drift downstream.

Wisps of his knife.
A horse tail in the clear blue morning
lifted toward the sky.

"How 'bout juice-can shoes for those prickly pears?"
the welder quips, as he makes an angle-iron axle.

My bolt-together cart
goes over curbs, through gravel, reeds, and mud.
He nods, and we agree.

"Even with these mountain bike tires that portage
will be tough. But this might work," he says.

Pieces lashed to the deck
near the chop-chop of the river, under bird
songs in the cottonwood.

Lewis had his prefab iron frames. I have my cart,
*The Journals*, and three farmers talking in a café:

"It's going to rain, I tell ya!" says the first.
"It's always going to rain," says the second.
"It sure looks like rain," says the third.

## Moths & Butterflies

sliding from streetlight
to star

words
seem tiny creatures

with hardly
any voice at all

their hushed presence
a mending flight

each petal aglow
far from the root

reflections
fluttering in the night

# The Passing of the Past

A gargoyle hovers
above traffic
warning of wreckage
in chrome and glass,
the trucks splashing past,
shrunk by the dark
waters of asphalt.

Unmistakably, a street person
as still as a statue and as remote,
a skinny man sits
on top of a bus stop bench
leaning over the toes
of his sneakers.

Memories linger,
spilling like oranges into alleyways
widening to undo the edges
of puddles. His unattached
cautionary tale freed
from its spinning wheel.

Other opinions
cross those parallels of loss,
and clouds go out of harmony
to comprise the sky.

So why not I?

## Streetwise, Riverwise

Weighed down by a city,
by a city that strangles trees,
he grew thinly green
fenced-in by iron spikes,
climbing curbsides,
lofted by the hum of concrete.
In the vast canyons of glass
he slid through grids
past mirrored squares
of wrong way windows
reflecting his skeleton's escape,
tilting around corners
like a dried branch
clawing along a cliff,
his eyes venturing out
amid bright shoes.
In tiny cupped cracks
of a guttered street, he watched
the sieves drain the rain
toward piers where water
swirled beneath his feet to rest
near the jagged toes of a river's
ragged edges—its curious mind
merging with blank reason
into all the empty spaces,
and he became stronger
knowing he would join it,
and yet by knowing he knew
his joining would be slow.

# Portage at Great Falls

Ping pong balls
bounce stalk to stalk below a cliff—
moths in the meadow wind.

Reeds are hushed without any sense of time,
as I paddle from day to day, perhaps too far, or lost.

Up to my chin, my feet
feel down into a slippery bowl,
a nest of rounded rocks.

River rapids plunge five feet into white water, —
and farther up, the Great Falls step through a veil of spray.

I bolt up the cart,
items of use on the kayak seat:
water, and the repair kit.

Two mountain bike tires span ruts of a gumbo road,
a washed-out cattle trail winding up and up.

Prickly pears blossom,
bulge into huge orange petals, brightly tipped,
thick pads sharp with spikes.

My feet dig in, up and up out of the gorge, little
by little, fingers grasping dirt higher with each breath.

The cart follows, pulled
or turned sideways to rest at switchbacks
on the narrow ridge trail.

By evening, I can barely slip beneath a locked gate
to the powdery surface of a county gravel road.

From its broken mesa
the gorge stretches below, the Missouri River
a ribbon simply unraveling.

Exhausted, I camp in a dusty ditch, knowing
the next hill will look lower in the morning.

Rain showers trace the land
wetting sections, then drying for hours.
I plod in the dust

like an ox swaying with a Santa Fe tumbrel
parallel to a woman, who's curious to know who I am.

She owns some ranch land
and chats from her red pickup truck—
our six wheels crunching along.

By nightfall, I reach intersects and sidewalks to splurge
on a room, the kayak cart padlocked in the parking lot.

A bath unbends me,
restores years to my life, peels away grime,
turning aches inside out.

And there are no worries. No need to cache my gear
at Medicine River—the white grizzly has gone.

I walk to Rainbow
and Black Eagle Falls, then to Giant Springs
where the trout swirl into flowers,

or drift like blimps above the submerged garden,
weightless in those healing waters of long ago.

# City!

City! with your dark avenues!
City! with your wide boulevards!

There are few spaces
left to embrace your slick quiet
that slips away
into incoherent conversations
between road signs
carried on too far into the night.

Commuter traffic and pedestrians
vanish in the broken, slow-motion
of your decay, the homeless
wrapped in blankets and bundled
by the moon
on purposeless sidewalks.

When the sun rises
pigeons will peck the steel plates
beneath the feet of gray suits
like small ghosts
steaming above the grates,
and haunted by an underground
awakened by the subway.

City! with your dark alleyways!
City! with your wide boulevards!

Why do you insist
I am your shrunken name?

## My Cat

It's good to watch cats
racing across the street
into the belief of superstition
where we live with ladders,
rakes, pails, and cracks
on old salted sidewalks.

Yesterday, a woman asked,
"Does your cat really walk on a leash?"

"Sure," I said, "as long as I follow him."
His world is safe with me.

"It's good to be with cats," she said.
They open our eyes to other spaces.

# Paddling Into Beauty

As Lewis and Clark did,
I launch on July 10th without wind
into the hot surreal air,

lifted by silent reflections of a rippling orange oak,
suspended on the shards of a big blue sky.

Astonished geese
march in uniform into my camp—
the gentle company of birds.

A family's pickup truck drives down the pasture slope,
fishing poles connecting slow water to shade trees,

big trout swimming
through their minds and caddis flies
swarming like river stars.

I tow the kayak in thin wind, between ranch lands,
past colors that totally please.

The reds and bright reds:
a beetle, a thistle, and a restroom
sloshed with paint and trout blood.

In streaks, hail falls from the far clouds, yet none here
where the meadows step toward the mountain.

Red rocks, silver stone,
wild flowers holding both sides
of a distant winter.

At the town of Cascade, the rapids narrow, "The Long Misery"
beginning to end in a bubbling conversation.

# At Three Forks

My feet say,
"Don't hurry. Be here, do this,"
splashing like hooves.

Long moss flows over skulls of Crow,
the Blackfeet riding above on hidden ponies.

The Missouri River curves
over rocks hot with sun, slopes past
thick brush crackling with a touch.

At the Little Gates, I sew up my sneakers to last
another day or two, in shin deep water at Three Forks.

A trestle on one side,
a highway on the other. Both sides
a boisterous moon.

It plays hide-and-seek between trains and trucks
in purple nights with Rocky Mountain silhouettes.

The gentle deer-scent
along Jefferson River holds me back
behind the tiny hoof prints.

And there is no better sound, nor better moment. Each
step is in my body, slippery with snow melt.

Rapids bubble past
from willow shade to mountain shade
to pools of blue light.

Bears snuffle in the fog near Big Baldy Mountain
strip-mined into a red cone, puddling the moonlight.

While sandhill cranes
nest in wild circles of upstream grasses,
I repair the broken rudder.

With practice, I step lightly among striped garter snakes
foraging like freight trains in the underwater valleys.

With intimate hugs
they nudge beneath rocks for nymphs,
holding their snake breaths.

All day I walk, until evening falls into my mind,
reading *Lame Deer* in the last quiet light of sunset.

A little brown bat
climbs up and nestles head down
from the top of my sock.

My feet, the roots, little wings that flutter, petals
attached to the earth, and a vase for each small thing.

# Two Antiques

*—for Pickles, the cat*

A frail disk spins
on a velvet turntable
with gentle emotions
from its shiny metal arm.

Morning always
closes the box
where the music had been,
the day a playground
circling and circling,
rising from its new place
like a kitten carried
in the dizziness of playing.

On spindly legs
we go round and round
captured by the vanishing,
disappearing
into the silence like a secret.

Waves are salty,
a horseshoe crab our pet
behind the shower curtain
on lots of scratchy feet,
like spiky seaweed
over milky porcelain.

A needle
goes up and down
above a singing machine
with its treadle seesaw
rocking all your dolls
furiously in a cave of legs.
The color of drapes

spins from the bobbin,
flashing past on its flat sash
to cross between the lines

as safely as if walking
across the street
from front porch to beach,
past clouds of fiddler crabs
on muddy flats
to coquinas rasping
in foamy footprints,
the waves hissing
beneath our feet
and the velvety blue sky
like magic, unfolding
the tide into a lacy froth.

## Bitterroot Flowers

Towing my way up
has been the best kind of doing
to climb those distant mountains.

Along cobblestone islands, the muskrats
whisper in a language now slightly familiar.

At the headwaters
the locals cast for lunkers,
seeking their secret pools,

a strong current undercutting the bank—the river
becoming equal to its melting mountain.

In the cold, cut-throat
swim in clear blue-ribbon waters
turning pink with sunset.

Cattle low on both sides, hoof prints crowding the river,
the herd slipping through narrow corner gates.

My feet go splashing
through the suburbs of Dillon, Montana,
toward bitterroot flowers,

past houses, a weir, the kayak sliding on wet grass
of a lawn where I linger.

# Mr. Day

Mr. Day kept goats.
In the morning, he would lead
his knobby-headed pets
to the meadow, and padlock
their booted chains
to snow fence posts
near huge granite boulders
of flickering mica
where they would stand for hours,
hoof tips clicking, lips
nibbling entire forests of lichens
from valleys of intricate rock,
their eyes as moist
as wood turtles in a cold stream,
as deep as golden galaxies.

At dusk, he would walk them home
along a two-lane blacktop road,
stooping to pick things up
or just ambling past the wildflowers.
Entering a weathered barn
he'd drop any loose hardware,
broken tool, or raggedy cloth
into a tin pail nailed to the door,
and bring any shoes or sneakers
up to the back porch
where he'd chunk them
into a large cardboard box.

If you were lucky
you might find him
out on the wooden step
drinking a glass of spring water
and trying to match up pairs,
the goats munching fresh hay

and resting beneath
all the inconsequential
dilapidations.

# A Mountain Lily

A mountain lily
shines underfoot in the snow.
Life is this close.

# Acknowledgments

My thanks to the editors of the publications where poems first appeared, sometimes in earlier versions:

*About Place Journal*: "Paddling Into the Plains of the Lakota," and "At Three Forks"

*Abiko Annual*: "James Joyce!"

*Albatross*: "Considering Flight"

*Amethyst Review*: "The Missouri River Breaks"

*Blue Unicorn*: "Streetwise, Riverwise"

*The Ekphrastic Review*: "Eglise d'Auvers"

*Frogpond*: "A Mountain Lily"

*Hopewell Review: Indiana Governor's Awards*, "Uncle Lowell"

*North Dakota Quarterly*: "Surviving April on Sakakawea Lake" and "Renewal at New Town, Berthold Reservation"

*North of Oxford*: "Two Antiques"

*Plainsongs*: "When I Was a Child," "And Home Again," and "Paddling Into Beauty"

*Poetry Forum Journal*: "Dancing"

*Poetry Greece*: "A Geography of the Heart"

*Point Judith Light*: "Reflections"

*Psychpoetica*: "Changes"

*Pudding Magazine*: "Departing the Mandans" as "Departure from Washburn, North Dakota"

*Ship of Fools*: "City!"

*Slipstream*: "One Heart Moving"

*Third Wednesday*: "Bitterroot Flowers"

*Weber–The Contemporary West*: "A Truth"

---

With special thanks to the Fort Mandan State Park, Washburn, North Dakota, for hosting the launch of "Gander" back onto the Missouri River.

To Cornerstone Press, in particular Dr. Ross Tangedal, Ellie Atkinson, Brett Hill, Carolyn Czerwinski, Zoie Dinehart, and Nat Reiter.

To Bob, Patty, Chris, and Lenny McNeill for their welcoming friendship at Dillon, Montana.

And to Sandie Seeger for her editing suggestions and loving encouragement.

MARK B. HAMILTON is the author of *OYO: The Beautiful River* (2020) and *Confronting the Basilisk* (1993). He was born in Hartford, Connecticut, grew up in North Granby, and attended San Diego State University (BA, MA) and the University of Montana Writers Workshop (MFA).

Among his honors are: a Matthew Hansen Endowment for Wilderness Studies; an independent readership at the American Antiquarian Society; a literary fellowship at UCROSS; an honorary residency at the Center for Art & Ecology; and a position as Visiting Faculty in Research, Department of History, Portland State University. He is perhaps the only living person to have traced the entire Lewis and Clark route on their approximate time-table, traveling as they did by paddle and pack mule.

For more on the author, visit:
www.MarkBHamilton.WordPress.com

www.ingramcontent.com/pod-product-compliance
Lightning Source LLC
Chambersburg PA
CBHW031251120626
46545CB00007B/2764